AMIR
KHAN
UNAUTHORISED BIOGRAPHY

Paul Harrison

**www.raintreepublishers.co.uk**
Visit our website to find out more information about Raintree books.

To order:
☎ Phone 44 (0) 1865 888112
🗎 Send a fax to 44 (0) 1865 314091
💻 Visit the Raintree bookshop at www.raintreepublishers.co.uk to browse our catalogue and order online.

Editorial: Catherine Veitch
Design: Richard Parker and Q2A Solutions
Illustrations: Oxford Designers and Illustrators
Picture research: Mica Brancic
Production: Victoria Fitzgerald

Originated by DOT graphics Ltd
Printed and bound in China by CTPS

ISBN 978 1 4062 0955 6
12 11 10 09 08
10 9 8 7 6 5 4 3 2 1

**British Library Cataloguing in Publication Data**
Harrison, Paul
Amir Khan. – (Sport files)
796.8'3'092
A full catalogue record for this book is available from the British Library.

**Acknowledgements**
We would like to thank the following for permission to reproduce photographs: © Action Images pp. **18** (Steven Paston); **23** (Michael Regan); © Alamy/eStock Photo p. **6**; © Corbis pp. **13** (NewSport/Stefan Matzke), **14** and **15** (Reuters/ Steve Marcus), **16** (Reuters/Russell Boyce), **25** (Reuters/Goran Tomasevic), **26** (Reuters/ Phil Noble); © Getty Images pp. **5** (Alex Livesey), **7** (Laureus/Clive Rose), **9** (Christopher Lee), **17** (Tim Graham), **20** (John Gichigi), **21** (Julian Finney); © Photoshot/Talking Sport p. **11**; © Rex Features/View Pictures/Raf Makda p. **22**.

Cover photograph of Amir Khan reproduced with permission of ©Getty Images (John Gichigi).

Every effort has been made to contact copyright holders of material reproduced in this book. Any omissions will be rectified in subsequent printings if notice is given to the publishers.

# CONTENTS

Some words are printed in bold, **like this**. You can find out what they mean by looking in the glossary.

Amir Khan is one of the most exciting young boxers in Britain today. He was a successful **amateur** boxer when most people first noticed him at the Olympic games in 2004. After this competition he became a star. Amir turned **professional** the next year and his unbeaten record of fights suggests that in the future he may become one of the most famous boxers ever!

Amir's fame has gone beyond boxing. He has also become a **role model**, not only for his sport, but for British Asians as well. This is because Amir is a **Muslim** and his family are originally from Pakistan (see map on page 12). Amir is proud of his background, but he is just as proud to represent Britain. This is one of the qualities that draws such strong support for Amir from the British public.

## FAST FACT FILE

| | |
|---|---|
| **Name:** | Amir Khan |
| **Born:** | 8 December 1986, Bolton |
| **Height:** | 1.78 m (5 ft 8) |
| **Weight:** | 63 kg (132 lbs) |
| **Boxing category:** | Lightweight |
| **Amateur titles:** | World Junior Champion |
| | European Youth Champion |
| | European Cadet Champion |
| | International Junior Olympic Champion |
| | ABA National Junior Champion |
| **Professional titles:** | **Commonwealth Lightweight Champion** |
| | IBF **Inter-continental Light Welterweight Champion** |

*After Amir's success at the Olympic Games, he has gone on to win professional boxing matches too.*

## Keeping his feet on the ground

Amir grew up in Bolton and still lives there with his parents. Many successful young sportspeople move to the bright lights of London, but this doesn't interest Amir. He doesn't drink and the idea of going to nightclubs doesn't really appeal to him. Also, he is very close to his family and friends in Bolton, whom he trusts and depends on. His father, Shajaad, is also his manager and his uncle Tahir and sister Tabinda are also part of his team. With his family to keep him heading in the right direction, Amir can concentrate on his boxing.

As a **professional** athlete Amir must be careful how he lives his life. Although he can enjoy time with his friends and family, he also has to concentrate on his sport. However, before Amir took up boxing he sometimes got into trouble. Some of the things he did were dangerous. When he was just five years old he managed to climb onto the roof of his parents' house. Another time he was knocked down by a car after running onto the road. After this accident Amir had to go to hospital and his family were worried his leg wouldn't heal properly. Luckily, after a period of doing special stretching exercises, his leg healed.

Amir also got into trouble in other ways, such as being involved in fights at school. His parents were not very surprised. When he was younger, he had been asked to leave his nursery school because of his poor behaviour.

## Taking up boxing

By the time Amir was eight years old his parents had to come up with new ways to cope with his behaviour. His father, Shajaad, decided to put Amir's fighting to good use and took him along to Halliwell Boxing Club. Shajaad hoped that Amir's behaviour would change and that he would begin to do as he was told.

From the moment Amir entered the club he loved it. Like all young boxers, Amir didn't fight straight away. Instead he learned the basics of boxing – how to stand properly, how to stay balanced, and how to throw the different types of punches. He also improved his fitness by running, skipping, **shadow boxing**, and working with the **punch bag**.

*Amir uses a punch bag to practise his punches.*

*Amir and his proud parents, Falak and Shajaad, the night after his last amateur fight.*

## The long wait

Even though Amir loved the training and was allowed to **spar**, he wasn't allowed to fight, because he was too young. He would have to wait for his chance to fight in the boxing ring.

Amir was 11 years old when he had his first **amateur** boxing fight. By that time the Halliwell Boxing Club had closed down, but a new one had replaced it – the Bolton Lads Club. The fight took place in Stoke-on-Trent one evening after school. Amir's dad and two of his uncles, Tahir and Terry, took him to the fight, and one of the coaches from the Bolton Lads Club was there too.

Amir changed into his Bolton Lads Club boxing outfit of head guard, orange top, black shorts with an orange stripe down each side, and blue boxing gloves. While he waited, he also wore an orange gown, to keep warm. It must have been a proud, yet scary, time for Amir as the time dragged by until his fight. Finally, it was Amir's turn. He walked to the ring, put his gumshield in, and waited for the bell to signal the start of the fight.

## AMATEUR BOXING

Amateur boxers do not fight for prize money; instead they try to win titles.

The length of a fight depends on the age of the boxers. An adult boxing match lasts for four rounds of two minutes each. A junior match can last for as little as three rounds of a minute and a half each.

During the fight, points are awarded for scoring punches. These are punches that land on the head or body of the opponent. An opponent can also be knocked out, or a fight can be stopped by the **referee** if he thinks it is necessary. If one fighter is too far ahead on points, then the fight is also stopped.

*In international amateur boxing competitions one boxer always wears blue and the other boxer wears red.*

## First win

Amir was quite small for his age, so he wasn't surprised that his **opponent**, Mark Jones, was taller than him. Mark was also more experienced and had fought a couple of times already. Amir wasn't worried though. When the bell sounded to start the first round of the fight he went straight at his opponent and scored some good points. The same thing happened in the next two rounds. By the end of the fight Amir was ahead on points and was the winner. Amir was exhausted, but delighted. He also had a huge trophy to show for his efforts.

After that first fight Amir really caught the boxing bug. He would fight anyone, at any time, anywhere in the country. He won his first three fights, but then came up against some tough **opponents**. He shouldn't really have been fighting some of them, as they were either older than him or in the wrong **weight category**.

## Changing clubs

Amir's dad thought that another boxing club might be better for Amir so he joined Bury **Amateur** Boxing Club. It was run by Mick Jelley, and under his coaching Amir became better and fitter than before. Just as his father had hoped, boxing had also stopped Amir getting into trouble. He behaved at school, studied hard, and passed six GCSEs.

## Getting better

Amir's wins continued and he was soon becoming well known in the boxing world. Not every fight went Amir's way, though. He lost the first national final he boxed in, the under-13 championship, after a close fight. However, whenever he lost he just became more determined to succeed, and trained even harder to make himself a better boxer. Amir began to win national titles and was considered to be one of the outstanding junior boxers in the country.

By the time he was 16, Amir was desperate to box at one of the most important amateur events, the World Cadet Championships. Unfortunately, the **Amateur Boxing Association (ABA)** thought he was too young to go and sent him to compete in the Junior **Olympics** instead.

### AMIR'S AMATEUR TITLES

Amir started fighting in championship competitions in 2000. By the end of his amateur career in 2005, he had won an impressive number of titles:

- Three English Schools titles
- Three Junior ABA titles
- Junior Olympic champion
- European Cadet Champion
- European Junior Champion
- World Junior Champion

## Junior Olympics

The Junior Olympics were held in the United States that year. Amir did much better than any British boxer had ever done before. He won the gold medal and also beat the top boxer from the United States. If anyone had doubted Amir's talent before, they now had the proof that he was someone to watch.

*Amir boxes in an amateur international boxing match against Michael Evans from the United States.*

After his success in the Junior **Olympics**, Amir wanted to represent Britain in the main Olympics the following year. However, the **ABA** ruined Amir's plans again. According to the rules, Amir was old enough to fight, but the ABA were worried because he would be fighting grown men. The ABA were concerned that Amir was not experienced or strong enough to compete against men, rather than boys. They decided to send him to the Junior Cadet European Championships rather than to the Olympic Games.

## Proud to be British

Although he was pleased to be representing Britain again, Amir was not happy that he had been turned down from the Olympics. For the first time in his life he began to question his identity. After Amir had won the Junior Olympics, he had been approached by some Americans. They had been so impressed with his boxing that they suggested that Amir move to the United States and fight for them. Although it would have been a great opportunity, Amir didn't want to move to the United States. However, there was another option – he could fight for Pakistan. Amir's parents were from Pakistan and, under Olympic rules, Amir was allowed to fight for his parent's country. He did consider this, but Amir had been born and brought up in the United Kingdom. This was the country he wanted to represent.

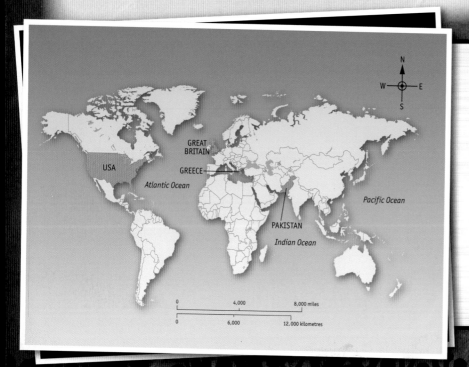

*This map shows four countries of great importance in the life of Amir Khan: Great Britain (his home); the United States (where he won the Junior Olympics); Greece (where he won the silver medal at the Athens Olympics); Pakistan (where his family originally came from).*

## Dream come true

Amir's only chance of getting to the Olympics was to let his boxing performances speak for themselves. Fortunately, Amir did very well at the Cadet Championships. Not only did he win his **weight category**, he was also voted boxer of the games. The ABA had no choice but to change their earlier decision and allow Amir to compete at the Olympic Games. However, even when a boxer is selected by their ABA, they still have to win international **qualifying fights** before they are allowed to represent their country. Amir was determined not to lose this opportunity and won his qualifying fights. He was going to the Olympics.

*The five joined rings on the Olympic flag represent the world's five continents.*

Amir was only 17 years old when he went to the 2004 **Olympics**. This made him the youngest boxer to represent Britain for over 30 years. In fact, that year he was the *only* boxer to represent Britain, as no other British boxer had been successful in their **qualifying fights**.

The 2004 Olympic Games were held in Athens, Greece (see map on page 12). The first boxer Amir faced was the Greek champion, Marios Kaperonis. There were many local supporters in the crowd, and the atmosphere was unlike anything Amir had ever experienced before. At first, it was hard for Amir to concentrate. When the bell rang for the start of the fight he seemed to forget everything he had been taught and boxed badly. However, he calmed down, and won the fight easily in the end.

*In the final bout, Cuban boxer Kindelan's experience was too much for Amir.*

## Good progress

Amir won his next two fights and was through to the semi-finals. By this time the British media were watching Amir's progress. He was surprised to see himself on sports programmes and he was asked many questions when he gave **press conferences**. Some of the most famous boxers of all time, such as Muhammad Ali and Lennox Lewis, had won an Olympic gold medal. Could Amir do the same?

In the semi-finals Amir struggled during the first two rounds of the fight. But he recovered well, to lead by the third round and take complete control in the final round. He was through to the final and would be guaranteed a medal.

Amir receives his Olympic silver medal at the 2004 Athens Olympics.

## The Olympic final

Amir's **opponent** in the final was a Cuban boxer called Mario Kindelan. He was one of the most experienced and respected boxers in the tournament. Amir was very nervous before the start of the fight. His nerves may have got the better of him, as Kindelan went into an early lead. It was a lead that Amir never recovered, and he was beaten. Amir had to be content with the silver medal.

After the **Olympics** Amir's life would never be the same again. If Amir felt disappointed by winning only a silver medal, those feelings were not shared by the British public – to them he was a hero. Amir was totally unprepared for the welcome he received when he flew back to Britain with the rest of the Olympic medal winners. Heathrow airport was packed with press and well-wishers, and Amir was surrounded by people asking questions or requesting autographs. The same was true when he flew into Manchester airport on his way back to Bolton. When he finally got home, it was the same again. In fact, there were so many people near his house that the roads were blocked.

The reason for Amir's popularity wasn't only because of his performance in the boxing ring. People liked Amir, they liked the good-looking, polite, hard-working young man. The fact that he was still at school also made a great story. Those next few days were a whirlwind for Amir. There were constant calls for interviews and photographs. The doorbell was always ringing, as people dropped by to pass on congratulations, or to ask for an autograph.

*Trafalgar Square was packed with crowds cheering the Olympic athletes, following a victory parade through London to celebrate their performance in Athens.*

## Amir the star

Amir was a celebrity now, so apart from all the interviews, there were also public engagements to attend. He was driven around Bolton in an open top bus and, along with the other successful Olympic athletes, Amir even met the Queen.

## Leaving school

Amir's success in the boxing ring was beginning to affect his everyday life. Amir was a student at Bolton Community College, where he was studying for a BTech in sports development and fitness. Trying to keep up with his boxing, as well as the studying, had been difficult enough before the Olympics, but now it was too much. Amir dropped out of school. His tutor said that he could return to the course if the boxing didn't work out. However, Amir seems to have abandoned the idea of going back to school now.

*Amir was chosen to help carry the baton holding the Queen's message of welcome part of the way to the 2006 Commonwealth Games in Melbourne.*

Amir had always planned to go to the 2008 **Olympics**. However, his success at the 2004 Olympic Games had made him very popular. Boxing promoters, the people who organize **professional** fights, wanted him to turn professional. This would be a big step. A professional boxer can earn a lot of money, but they can't fight at events such as the Olympics that are only open to **amateur** athletes. Did Amir want to try and get rich as a professional boxer, or did he want to win an Olympic gold?

Amir didn't rush into any decisions. He listened to what his family and coach had to say, and continued to box in amateur tournaments. Despite all the distractions, Amir progressed through to the quarter finals of the **ABA seniors**. Then the problems started.

## Falling out with the ABA

Tickets for popular boxing tournaments could sometimes be a problem. If an event was popular, free tickets given to the boxers for their friends and families, could be in short supply. Amir had requested 300 tickets for the quarter finals and thought that he had been promised that number. When the tournament arrived he only received 10; Amir's team was furious. As the issue didn't look like being resolved, Amir pulled out of that year's competition.

*Frank Warren (far right) helps to drum up publicity for Amir's fight with Graham Earl (far left).*

## AMATEUR AND PROFESSIONAL BOXING

There are a number of differences between amateur and professional boxing. There are no head guards in professional boxing, nor do professionals wear vest tops. The fights are also longer, lasting up to twelve rounds of three minutes each.

The way boxers fight in amateur and professional competition is also different. In amateur boxing, the fighters land punches in order to score points. In professional boxing, the fighters are awarded points for scoring punches, but they also try to stop their **opponents** by hitting them so hard they are unable to continue.

The other major differences are that professional boxers fight for prize money and champions in different weight divisions are awarded belts, rather than trophies.

## Last amateur fight

The relationship between Amir and the **ABA** was now difficult. Things got worse when Amir wanted to have a rematch with Mario Kindelan. Amir felt that the ABA was trying to prevent the fight from taking place. When the fight finally did happen, it was seen live on television by millions of people. As they watched him win, most viewers didn't realise that they had seen Amir's last amateur fight. He had signed a contract with the boxing promoter Frank Warren. Amir was turning professional.

Turning **professional** meant that Amir's successful relationship with his coach Mick Jelley had to end. The different skills required for professional boxing meant it was time for a new gym and a new trainer. Working with the right person was really important – it could mean the difference between success and failure. Frank Warren helped Amir find the right person and introduced him to Oliver Harrison. The two men took an instant liking to each other, and a new team was born.

*Oliver Harrison puts Amir through his paces during training at the Peacock Gym in London before Amir's fight with Daniel Thorne.*

## Building up fitness

Professional boxers need to build up their stamina, so they can last the length of each fight. Oliver trains boxers for this with the help of a horizontal metal bar and a **punch bag**. The bar is set about a metre above the ground. The boxer has to jump over it, keeping their knees and ankles together. After a minute of this, they move on to the punch bag and then back to the bar again. It sounds easy enough, but it is exhausting.

Amir also had to relearn how to throw a punch. In **amateur** boxing the aim is just to land a blow to score a point. In the professional sport, the aim is to stop an **opponent**, so the punches have to be harder. Oliver helped Amir improve his technique.

## Icy surprise

Many of the other exercises Amir did with Oliver were familiar. There was bag work, **sparring**, running, skipping, as well as work on the pads, where the boxer hits pads that the trainer holds. However, Oliver had one more unpleasant surprise – ice baths! After a tough workout the boxer sits in a freezing cold bath for a few minutes. This is supposed to help the body to recover and prevent injury. So far Amir has avoided serious injury, so maybe it works!

Hard though this training was, there was a definite goal in sight. Amir's first professional fight was set for 6 July 2005. It was to be against the boxer, David Bailey, and was due to take place in Amir's home town of Bolton. But as the fight drew near, national events overshadowed it, and threw Amir's background and religion into the spotlight.

*Amir and Oliver celebrate after yet another successful fight. Amir defended his Commonwealth Light Championship title against Graham Earl in December 2007. He won it in the first round with a technical knockout.*

Amir is one of the most famous **Muslims** in Britain today. Although he has a hectic life, he tries to stick to the rules and regulations laid down by his faith. This can help him but it can also cause problems for him as a **professional** athlete. For example, as a Muslim, Amir doesn't drink and this is good for his training. On the other hand, more care needs to be taken during Ramadan, a holy month for Muslims, when they are expected to **fast** during daylight hours. During this period it can be difficult if Amir needs to train hard for an upcoming fight. He has to make sure he eats enough food before dawn to last him until sunset, when he can eat again. The only time Amir breaks his fast is if he has to fight during Ramadan.

Unfortunately, following terrorist attacks in Britain and the United States, the Muslim religion has come under the spotlight for all the wrong reasons. Amir's popularity is a refreshing contrast to some of the negative images that have arisen. Amir makes sure that he is seen as being both a proud Muslim, and a proud British citizen. Like most Muslims, he does not believe that his religion supports terrorist violence. After the bomb attacks in London in July 2005 he felt that it was important for people to see that Muslims were not a threat to the country.

*Muslims worship at a building called a mosque. Muslims attend prayers at a mosque every Friday.*

*Amir with David Bailey, the boxer he fought in his first professional fight. Sadly, tragic events overshadowed the fight.*

## The first fight

Amir was due to have his first professional fight nine days after the terrorist attacks in London, in which 56 people died. On the day of the fight, when he walked out to the ring, he carried the Union Jack with the word "London" written across the middle. Friends in the crowd waved flags that were half Union Jack and half Pakistan. When the fight was over, Khan dedicated his win to the victims of the bombings. Amir had made his point, simply and effectively.

Amir knows how the attention he receives can be used to make a difference to other people's lives. He has spent a lot of time and money helping out many good causes. In 2005 there was a huge earthquake in Pakistan. Many people died and around three million people were left homeless. As many of Amir's relatives still live in Pakistan, he felt he had to do something. He raised money for the victims of the earthquake and even went to visit the devastated area. He was both shocked and touched by what he saw there. This made him even more determined to keep the story in the news so that more money might be raised.

Closer to home, Amir has also been an **ambassador** for the National Society for the Prevention of Cruelty to Children (NSPCC). He made himself available for interviews in order to publicize their "Full Stop" campaign to end cruelty. Amir felt honoured to be asked. He was already a supporter of the NSPCC, and being able to use his fame to help them was a good feeling.

Amir also starred in a television series called *Angry Young Men*. The aim of the series was to give some youngsters the opportunity to get their lives in order, by training with Amir and seeing how he lived his life. It gave the young men who took part a way of using their energy positively and it tried to give them a better understanding of right and wrong. This had worked for Amir, but only time could tell if his example would work for others.

## GIVING SOMETHING BACK

Amir has spent hundreds of thousands of pounds of his own money converting an empty building in a rundown part of Bolton into a gym, containing all the latest equipment. The Gloves Community Centre, as it is called, opened in January 2008. The entrance fee for the centre is very low, so that local youths can go there to train, get fit, or just hang out. There will also be a computer and homework rooms. But Amir's other dream for his gym is that it produces another successful boxer.

In Muzaffarabad, a region in the north of Pakistan, Amir met some young survivors of the terrible earthquake.

Like all amateur boxers, Amir had to be eased into the **professional** game. As long as both boxers agree, fights can be arranged over any length. To help Amir adjust to longer rounds, Frank Warren arranged for Amir's first six fights to be scheduled for four rounds only. But Amir usually beat his **opponents** before the last round anyway.

## Amir's first belt

As Amir improved, Frank arranged fights with more skilful opponents. With each fight, Amir got better and learned a little bit more about how to box professionally. By his seventh fight Amir was undefeated, so Frank increased the length of the fights to six rounds. By his tenth contest, the fight was ten rounds long and Amir was fighting for his first belt, the International Boxing Federation **inter-continental light welterweight title**.

*Amir has successfully defended his Commonwealth Lightweight title.*

Normally Amir fought in the lightweight division, which is for boxers weighing up to 63 kilograms. However, in order to gain experience, Amir was forced to go up a category temporarily for this fight. Many boxers find going up a **weight category** fairly easy. Most of the time boxers are naturally a little bit heavier than their fighting weight and lose weight as they train. But Amir is naturally a lightweight, so going up a weight was more of a challenge for him. Amir survived the longer distance and the judges awarded him the fight.

## Another belt

It was not long before Amir added another, more important, belt to his collection – the **Commonwealth Lightweight title**. On 14 July 2007 Amir fought the title-holder, Willie Limond, a Scottish boxer with a good reputation. It was a hard fight, and Amir was knocked down in the sixth round. He fought back, though, and stopped Limond in the eighth round.

Amir remained undefeated in his first seventeen professional fights. Then in a major shock, Amir spilt from his trainer, Oliver Harrison, in April 2008. It seems that Amir's team believed he needed a new trainer to take Amir to the next level and a **World Championship belt**.

Amir has sacrificed much to get where he is. Fortunately his family are very supportive. He also has close friends he can relax with. From this solid base who knows how far Amir will go?

## WHO AWARDS PROFESSIONAL BELTS?

Professional boxing is controlled by a number of rival organizations, including the International Boxing Federation, the World Boxing Organization, the World Boxing Association, and the World Boxing Council. They each have their own champions and rank boxers as to their ability. They also decide who should challenge for belts. Boxers can compete for any or all of the organizations' belts and many boxers aim to win all four of the major association titles. This is called unifying the title.

| | |
|---|---|
| **8 December 1986** | Amir is born in Bolton, Lancashire. |
| **12 December 1997** | Amir's first **amateur** fight. |
| **28 April 2001** | Amir wins the National Youth Championship. |
| **10 March 2002** | Amir wins the **ABA** Youth Championship. |
| **6 July 2002** | Amir wins the Four Nations Cadet Championship. |
| **10 May 2003** | Amir wins the National Juniors Finals. |
| **24 May 2003** | Amir wins the ABA National Juniors Finals. |
| **3 July 2003** | Amir wins the Junior **Olympics.** |
| **9 August 2003** | Amir wins the European Cadet Championship. |
| **15 November 2003** | Amir wins the European Youth Championship. |
| **18 June 2004** | Amir wins the World Junior Championship. |
| **29 August 2004** | Amir wins an Olympic silver medal. |
| **14 May 2005** | Amir's last amateur fight – a win against Mario Kindelan. |
| **16 July 2005** | Amir wins his first **professional** fight. |
| **9 December 2006** | Amir wins the IBF **inter-continental light welterweight belt**. |
| **17 July 2007** | Amir wins a **Commonwealth lightweight** belt. |
| **October 2007** | Amir successfully defends his Commonwealth lightweight title with a fourth-round stoppage against Scott Lawton at the Nottingham Arena. |
| **December 2007** | Amir scores the most significant victory of his career with a magnificent first-round knockout of British number one Graham Earl at the Bolton Arena. |
| **10 January 2008** | Official opening of Amir's Gloves Community Centre. |
| **2 February 2008** | Amir retains his Commonwealth lightweight title with a unanimous points win over Australian Gairy St Clair. |
| | Amir defends his Commonwealth title. |

# FACT FILE

- Amir's favourite boxer is Muhammad Ali.

- One of Amir's cousins is Saj Mahmood, the England cricketer.

- Amir went to the same school as the cricketer Ronni Irani, actor Paul Nicholls, and the comedian Dave Spikey.

- Amir was good at running, and some of his teachers thought he could have been an athlete if he hadn't become a boxer.

- Amir supports Bolton Wanderers Football Club and was once invited into the changing rooms before a match to give the team a pep talk.

- Haroon, Amir's younger brother, has followed Amir into the ring and is also a good **amateur** boxer.

- Amir has visited the city of Mecca in Saudi Arabia – the holiest site in the **Muslim** religion.

- Amir's first car was a brand new Range Rover. He bought it before he passed his driving test, when he was 17 years old.

# GLOSSARY

**ABA seniors** annual, national competition for amateur boxers aged 17 and over

**amateur** someone who plays their sport as a pastime, rather than as their job

**Amateur Boxing Association (ABA)** organization that organizes and controls amateur boxing

**ambassador** someone who represents an organization or country

**Commonwealth lightweight title** competition open to boxers weighing up to 63 kilograms, and who come from countries that are members of the British Commonwealth

**fast** to go without food and drink for a time

**inter-continental light welterweight title** competition open to boxers weighing up to 63.5 kilograms

**Muslim** follower of Islam, a religion based on the teachings of the prophet Mohammad

**Olympics** sporting event held every four years made up of a series of different athletic competitions. Competitors must be amateurs.

**opponent** person a boxer fights against

**press conference** event where journalists can ask a person questions

**professional** someone who gets paid to play their sport

**punch bag** large, stuffed, heavy bag that boxers hit when exercising

**qualifying fights** series of fights that a boxer must win to prove that they are good enough to compete in a future boxing event

**referee** person who stands in the ring with the boxers during a fight to make sure that both boxers are following the rules

**role model** person who is a good example to others

**shadow boxing** exercise where boxers throw lots of different punches at an imaginary opponent

**spar** practice fights where the boxers try not to hurt each other

**weight category** boxers are put into different categories according to their weight so that they can fight other boxers of a similar weight to themselves.

**World Championship belt** international title awarded to the best boxer in a particular weight category

## Books

*A Boy from Bolton: My Story*, Amir Khan (Bloomsbury, 2006)

*A World-Class Boxer*, Don Wood (Heinemann Library, 2005)

## Websites

http://www.aiba.org/
The website of the International Amateur Boxing Association has all the latest news and rankings.

http://www.amirkhan-boxing.com/
Learn more about Amir on his official website. Find out when his next fight is and see the results of all his fights.

http://www.amirsfans.co.uk/
Find out more information about Amir at the official fan site.

http://www.frankwarren.tv/
Lots of information about boxing and upcoming fights.

### Disclaimer

All the Internet addresses (URLs) given in this book were valid at the time of going to press. However, due to the dynamic nature of the Internet, some addresses may have changed, or sites may have changed or ceased to exist since publication. While the author and Publishers regret any inconvenience this may cause readers, no responsibility for any such changes can be accepted by either the author or the Publishers. It is recommended that adults supervise children on the Internet.